Faith FOR TOUGH TIMES

*A 4-week course to help
senior highers understand how
faith can help them deal with
difficult situations*

by David Cassady

Group
Loveland, Colorado

Group®

Faith for Tough Times
Copyright © 1991 by Group Publishing, Inc.

Credits
Edited by Stephen Parolini
Cover designed by Jill Christopher and DeWain Stoll
Interior designed by Judy Bienick and Jan Aufdemberge
Illustrations by Raymond Medici
Cover photo by David Priest
Photo on p. 28 by Gene Plaisted

ISBN 1-55945-216-1

14 13 12 11 10 9 8   04 03 02 01 00 99 98
Printed in the United States of America.

CONTENTS

96943

FAITH FOR TOUGH TIMES

The blaring sirens were lost in the roaring of the wind and the sound of debris crashing into the house. Sarah made another futile attempt to crawl even farther into the corner of the closet where she'd taken shelter.

As the violent clamor of the storm swirled all around her, her mind was focused on her parents: "Where were they? Were they safe?" She also worried about her friends two houses down. Had the tornado caught them by surprise?

Sarah prayed and shivered until the storm passed. When she emerged from the closet, it was to a different house. The wind had rearranged the furniture, broken the windows and created a gaping hole in the roof. It felt strange to feel rain-drops in the living room.

She ran outside and toward her friends' house. In horror she froze on the sidewalk, for all that remained of their house was rubble and a slab of concrete. As her heart broke, she cried out to God, "Why!?"

● ● ●

It's tough growing up today, maybe tougher than any previous time. Kids are trying to decide who they are, what they believe and what's valuable in life. Such issues are hard enough by themselves but even more complicated when a tragedy strikes close to home, when friends reject kids' acts of faith or when they're confronted with the dark cavern of depression. Teenagers must face many "scary" times in today's world. The strength of a senior higher's faith will likely be tested by such events and pressures. But the risk of thinking about such "tough times" is more than offset by the teachable moments created.

Disasters—such as that Sarah faced—can be times of intense questioning about God and faith. How such questions are handled can make a difference in faith being made stronger or weaker. Senior highers want to face these issues and questions head-on, and they need straight talk from Christian leaders. Our honesty in sharing our own faith struggles can help kids see that tragedy is a normal part of life.

Another tough thing for kids is depression. Senior highers are going through strong internal

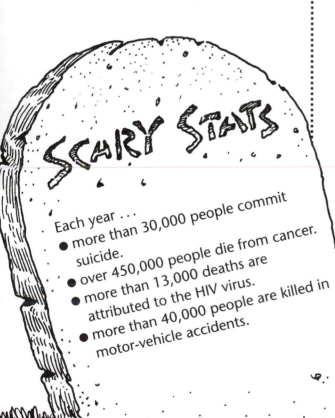

SCARY STATS

Each year . . .
● more than 30,000 people commit suicide.
● over 450,000 people die from cancer.
● more than 13,000 deaths are attributed to the HIV virus.
● more than 40,000 people are killed in motor-vehicle accidents.

struggles about values, purpose and identity. Simultaneously, their bodies are churning with rapid growth. Hormones confuse their senses and their judgment. Mood swings are common and can be extreme. A depressed teenager can begin to believe that no one—including God—cares or understands. We can help kids find support in Christian peers and in the always-present love of Christ.

Sometimes kids act on their Christian values only to be picked on or ridiculed by their peers. Such persecution is not only painful but can inhibit a young faith. Senior highers want to know how to be Christians and how to handle those who don't understand.

Faith is alive in all Christians, and faith can be nurtured, enriched and made stronger. Helping senior highers gain stronger faith means asking tough questions. Then when tough times come, kids will know that their faith can be a help and not a burden.

By the end of this course your students will:
- struggle with the feelings, questions and issues that arise when they come upon "tough times";
- discover how the Bible is full of feelings and issues that can help them in tough times;
- find encouragement and confidence that their faith can survive depression, persecution or tragedy;
- develop skills to cope with disasters, depression and persecution;
- examine the importance of building a strong faith; and
- explore ways to exercise their faith.

COURSE OBJECTIVES

HOW TO USE THIS COURSE

Think back on an important lesson you've learned in life. Did you learn it from reading about it? from hearing about it? from something you experienced? Chances are, the most important lessons you've learned came from something you experienced. That's what active learning is—learning by doing. And active learning is a key element in Group's Active Bible Curriculum.

Active learning leads students in doing things that help them understand important principles, messages and ideas. It's a discovery process that helps kids internalize what they learn.

Each lesson section in Group's Active Bible Curriculum plays an important part in active learning:

The **Opener** involves kids in the topic in fun and unusual ways.

The **Action and Reflection** includes an experience designed to evoke specific feelings in the students. This section also processes those feelings through "How did you feel?" questions and applies the message to situations kids face.

The **Bible Application** actively connects the topic with the Bible. It helps kids see how the Bible is relevant to the situations they face.

The **Commitment** helps students internalize the Bible's message and commit to make changes in their lives.

The **Closing** funnels the lesson's message into a time of creative reflection and prayer.

When you put all the sections together, you get a lesson that's fun to teach—and kids get messages they'll remember.

● Read the Introduction, the Course Objectives and This Course at a Glance.

● Decide how you'll publicize the course using the art on the Publicity Page (p. 9). Prepare fliers, newsletter articles and posters as needed.

● Look at the Bonus Ideas (p. 46) and decide which ones you'll use.

● Read the opening statements, Objectives and Bible Basis for the lesson. The Bible Basis shows how specific passages relate to senior highers today.

● Choose which Opener and Closing options to use. Each is appropriate for a different kind of group. The first option is often more active.

● Gather necessary supplies from This Lesson at a Glance.

● Read each section of the lesson. Adjust where necessary for your class size and meeting room.

BEFORE EACH LESSON

● The approximate minutes listed give you an idea of how long each activity will take. Each lesson is designed to take 35 to 60 minutes. Shorten or lengthen activities as needed to fit your group.

● If you see you're going to have extra time, do an activity or two from the "If You Still Have Time . . ." box or from the Bonus Ideas (p. 46).

● Dive into the activities with the kids. Don't be a spectator. The lesson will be more successful and rewarding to both you and your students.

HELPFUL HINTS

● The answers given after discussion questions are responses your students *might* give. They aren't the only answers or the "right" answers. If needed, use them to spark discussion. Kids won't always say what you wish they'd say. That's why some of the responses given are negative or controversial. If someone responds negatively, don't be shocked. Accept the person, and use the opportunity to explore other angles of the issue.

THIS COURSE AT A GLANCE

Before you dive into the lessons, familiarize yourself with each lesson aim. Then read the scripture passages.
- Study them as a background to the lessons.
- Use them as a basis for your personal devotions.
- Think about how they relate to teenagers' circumstances today.

LESSON 1: WHY DO BAD THINGS HAPPEN?

Lesson Aim: To help teenagers see how faith helps them respond to tragic times or events.

Bible Basis: Ecclesiastes 8:16-17; 9:11-12; and John 9:1-7.

LESSON 2: WHEN OTHERS LAUGH AT YOU

Lesson Aim: To help teenagers learn how to respond to people who ridicule them or hassle them because of their faith.

Bible Basis: Daniel 3:8-30 and Acts 16:20-35.

LESSON 3: WHEN YOU FEEL DOWN

Lesson Aim: To help teenagers understand how faith can help them when they feel down.

Bible Basis: Lamentations 3:19-24 and Matthew 26:36-39.

LESSON 4: THE SUPER FAITH WORKOUT

Lesson Aim: To help teenagers discover ways to strengthen their faith so they can better face tough times.

Bible Basis: Psalm 46 and Ephesians 6:10-18.

PUBLICITY PAGE

Grab your senior highers' attention! Copy this page, then cut and paste the art of your choice in your church bulletin or newsletter to advertise this course on *Faith for Tough Times*. Or copy and use the ready-made flier as a bulletin insert. Permission to photocopy clip art is granted for local church use.

Splash this art on posters, fliers or even post-cards! Just add the vital details: the date and time the course begins, and where you'll meet.

It's that simple.

THE DAILY BLAH

FAITH FOR TOUGH TIMES

TORNADO HITS SMALL TOWN!

A 4-week high school course to help you deal with tragedy, ridicule and depression

Come to _____

On _____

At _____
_____

Come learn how a strong faith can help you face tough times!

WHY DO BAD THINGS HAPPEN?

Teenagers ask a lot of "why" questions as they grow into adulthood. But one of the toughest questions they ask is "Why do bad things happen to good people?" It's a tough question without an easy answer. Tough questions like this one may lead kids to question God. Yet instead of questioning God, kids can learn to respond in faith to tragedies.

To help teenagers see how faith helps them respond to tragic times or events.

LESSON AIM

Students will:
- experience examples of tragedies and discuss why bad things happen;
- discover how the Bible can help them respond to tragedy;
- brainstorm responses to tragic situations; and
- explore how they can be God's healing hands for people who suffer tragedies.

OBJECTIVES

Look up the following scriptures. Then read the background paragraphs to see how the passages relate to your senior highers.

In **Ecclesiastes 8:16-17; 9:11-12**, the author tries to understand why bad things happen to good people.

In this passage, the philosopher is struggling with a "why" question about life. He wonders why things happen that people can't control. He concludes in Ecclesiastes 8:17 that even wise people cannot know why some things happen.

Teenagers also try to figure out how the world works and why things happen. But just as the writer of Ecclesiastes

BIBLE BASIS
ECCLESIASTES 8:16-17; 9:11-12
JOHN 9:1-7

discovered, kids soon realize they can't understand everything about how the world works. Instead, they can focus on what they can do in response to problems.

In **John 9:1-7**, the disciples ask Jesus why a certain man was born blind.

In this passage, the disciples seem more interested in knowing what caused the man's blindness than how they ought to respond to the man. Jesus shows that such tragedies are opportunities to do the healing work of God and thus show God's glory.

Senior highers often want to know whose fault tragedies are. But teenagers can learn to respond to tough times not by asking "Why?" as the disciples did but by asking "What can I do to heal?" as Jesus did.

THIS LESSON AT A GLANCE

Section	Minutes	What Students Will Do	Supplies
Opener (Option 1)	5 to 10	**All Torn Up**—Tear a folded list of important things.	Paper, pencils
(Option 2)		**Spilt Milk**—Deal with the problem of a spilled drink.	Soft drink, towel
Action and Reflection	15 to 20	**Big Trouble**—Play a simulation about cities in crisis.	"Big Trouble" handouts (p. 18), scissors, 3×5 cards, pencils
Bible Application	10 to 15	**Responding to Tragedy**—Examine scriptures that deal with senseless suffering.	Bibles
Commitment	5 to 10	**Where's the Glue?**—Brainstorm faith responses to tragic situations.	"Where's the Glue?" handouts (p. 19), pencils
Closing (Option 1)	up to 5	**God's Toolbox**—See themselves as tools for God's healing work.	Masking tape
(Option 2)		**Heart Repair**—Repair torn sheets of paper.	Torn paper from All Torn Up, paper, clear tape

The Lesson

Note: This lesson may bring up powerful feelings in your kids. You may find kids who actually feel angry at God for tragedies they've experienced or been close to. Be sensitive to kids who feel this way; they may be angry because of a sense of loss or confusion. Help them understand we *don't* understand everything that happens, but we can trust God in even the most difficult times.

☐ OPTION 1: ALL TORN UP

Give kids each a sheet of paper and a pencil. Ask teenagers each to write on the paper the names of people or things that are important or valuable to them. Tell them they can write these things anywhere on the paper.

Then ask the kids each to fold their paper in half four times. They should end up with a small rectangle. Say: **Sometimes things or people like the ones we listed are taken from us by disasters or accidents.**

Have kids each tear their folded paper in half and choose one half to keep. Collect the other halves. Have kids open their papers to see what people or items they "lost" in the disaster.

Then ask:

● **How many valuable things or important people did you list?** (A bunch; a few; none.)

● **If you lost something or somebody, what or who was it?** (My stereo; my best friend; a family member.)

● **How'd you feel when you realized your loss?** (It was unfair; I was relieved it wasn't my parents; I was angry.)

● **How is this activity like real life when people are affected by disasters or tragedies around them?** (People are upset about losses in real life; people do lose friends or family in real life.)

Say: **It's tough to make sense of tragedies that strike innocent people. And it's normal to wonder why God lets tragedies happen. But when finding an answer is difficult, people still need our help. Today we'll begin to discover how we can respond with our faith to tragedies.**

Have kids save their torn papers if you plan on using Closing (Option 2): Heart Repair.

☐ OPTION 2: SPILT MILK

Bring a soft drink into the room, and sip it while kids arrive. When you're ready to begin the class, "accidently" spill the drink on the floor. Then, instead of immediately cleaning it up, begin asking "why" questions such as "Why did this have to happen today?" or "Why did this have to happen to

OPENER
(5 to 10 minutes)

me?" Go overboard with your anger about having spilled your drink. Be sure you have kids' attention. Some may try to offer suggestions about why this happened or tell you not to worry about it. After a minute or two, stop carrying on and use a towel to clean up the mess.

After you clean up the mess, ask:

● **How'd you feel about the way I responded after spilling my drink?** (I thought it was funny; I was confused; I was surprised.)

● **How is my response like a response people have to disasters or tragedies?** (People ask why tragedies happen; people can't respond to the tragedy because they're too busy being upset by it.)

● **What might've been a better response to my "tragedy"?** (Just clean up the mess; not worry about the spill.)

Say: **A spilled drink is a microscopic inconvenience compared to tragedies that shake the world such as tornadoes, earthquakes and hurricanes. Many of you may know someone who's died from cancer or in an accident. These events may cause you to wonder why God allows these things to happen.**

It's okay to ask about such things—it's natural to question why bad things happen. But as with the spilled drink, we need to learn how to get beyond the "why" questions and discover how we can respond to the people affected by the tragedy.

Today we'll begin to uncover ways to deal with bad things that happen to good people.

ACTION AND REFLECTION
(15 to 20 minutes)

BIG TROUBLE

Have kids form a circle. Say: **For the next few minutes, each of you will become a mayor of a major city. You'll each receive a description of your city. The description includes whether a disaster has befallen your city and what your reaction to the disaster (or lack of it) will be. Read your description, and then talk with other mayors as you try to meet the goal described on your handout.**

Give kids each one of the Mayor's Report boxes cut apart from the "Big Trouble" handout (p. 18). Be sure at least one of each box is distributed. Distribute an equal number of each Mayor's Report box among your group.

On "go," have kids each read their Mayor's Report and go around talking with other cities' mayors. Every minute or so, announce that another 25 to 100 people have died or are homeless in the disaster-ridden cities. After five to six minutes, end the simulation.

Then ask:

● **How'd you feel as you read your city's situation?** (Confident; angry; frustrated; disappointed; relieved.)

● **If your city had just experienced a disaster, how'd you feel?** (It was unfair; I didn't like it; I knew it'd happen to me.)

● **What did you learn about other mayors as you talked with them?** (Some mayors didn't want to help; some were more concerned with why the disaster happened than what to do about it.)

● **How'd you feel about the role you played?** (I'd rather have been able to help; I felt silly; I liked my role.)

● **How are the mayors' responses to tragedies like the responses you have to tragedies?** (We all have different responses; sometimes I ask "why?"; disasters don't bother me much.)

● **What did you learn from this simulation that could help you deal with tragedies?** (We need to help each other; we need to put other's needs above our own.)

Say: **The tragedies we used for this simulation are the kind we hear about in the news. But smaller tragedies closer to home can actually seem pretty big too.**

Give kids each a 3×5 card and a pencil. Have kids each write one or more tragedies that affect people on a personal level. Kids might list things such as people dying from cancer; innocent victims of gang violence; or accident victims. Collect and read aloud the cards.

Ask:

● **Why do these things happen?** (God lets them happen; people make them happen; I don't know.)

Say: **We don't always know why things happen, but we can learn how to respond to tragedies such as these. Let's look at the Bible for guidance on how to respond.**

RESPONDING TO TRAGEDY

Form two groups, and assign each group a different passage: Ecclesiastes 8:16-17; 9:11-12; or John 9:1-7.

Have groups each read their passage and choose someone to be the "voice" for their group. Say: **I'm going to ask a few questions. After I ask a question, groups each may briefly discuss the question before your voice answers it as if he or she were the author of your scripture passage. In other words, your voice will answer the question aloud as the author of your passage might've answered it if he or she were with us today.**

Ask groups each the following questions:

● **How should we respond to tragedies?** (We shouldn't just ask why; we should try to help in the healing process; we should trust God to take care of us.)

● **What role does faith play in dealing with unexpected circumstances?** (We have to trust that God is in control; our faith helps us overcome difficult times; our faith helps us respond to others in need.)

● **How would you respond to someone whose close friend or family member dies from cancer?** (I'd tell him or her we can't understand everything, but we're willing to help in any way we can; I'd tell him or her to trust God to help get past the anger and pain.)

BIBLE APPLICATION
(10 to 15 minutes)

● **How would you respond to a community that's devastated by a hurricane?** (I'd try to get them to see how faith can help them deal with the situation; I wouldn't know how to respond; I'd help raise money to send to the people in need.)

Thank the voices for helping with this activity. Then form a circle and ask:

● **Which of the mayors in the simulation we participated in earlier was most like your passage?** (The questioning role was like Ecclesiastes; the cities that helped were kind of like Jesus helping the blind man.)

● **Which passage helps us see how we should respond to crises? Explain.** (The passage in John, because it shows how we can help people who've been affected by tragedy; the passage in Ecclesiastes, because it shows how we can't know why and must rely on faith.)

Say: **Jesus shows us a faith that heals. Like the disciples and the writer of Ecclesiastes, we can begin to see how our faith can help others deal with tragedy.**

COMMITMENT
(5 to 10 minutes)

WHERE'S THE GLUE?

Give kids each a "Where's the Glue?" handout (p. 19) and a pencil. Have kids each complete their handout. Then form groups of no more than five. Have kids share their suggestions from their handouts and discuss ways they can use their faith to deal with tragedies and difficult situations.

Form a circle, and have representatives from each group share ideas they discussed from their handouts. Then have kids commit to using the ideas they came up with when dealing with tragedies or other bad things that happen to people they know.

Say: **By learning to rely on our faith in tough times, we'll grow closer to God and learn to trust him.**

Table Talk

The Table Talk activity in this course helps senior highers talk with their parents about how faith can help them in tough times.

If you choose to use the Table Talk activity, this is a good time to show students the "Table Talk" handout (p. 20). Ask them to spend time with their parents completing it.

Before kids leave, give them each the "Table Talk" handout to take home, or tell them you'll be sending it to their parents.

Or use the Table Talk idea found in the Bonus Ideas (p. 46) for a meeting based on the handout.

☐ OPTION 1: GOD'S TOOLBOX

Form a circle. Say: **Sometimes we forget that God has chosen us to be a part of his healing work in this world. When people feel discouraged or angry because of tragedies in their lives, we can reach out in faith to help them in God's name.**

Stand before each teenager and take his or her right hand. Say: **In God's hands, you're a tool for repairing the broken places in this world.**

Then place a piece of masking tape on the back of his or her hand. Do this for each teenager, and look them each in the eyes while you say the words.

Have kids hold hands as you close with prayer, asking God to use each person in his healing work. Encourage kids each to keep their strip of masking tape with them during the next week—as a reminder of the faith that helps others in times of despair.

☐ OPTION 2: HEART REPAIR

If you used All Torn Up, skip the next paragraph and go right to the paragraph below it. Be sure kids each have their torn paper from the opener (including the half you collected).

Give kids each a sheet of paper. Have kids each write their name on the paper. Go around and tear each person's paper in half, saying: **When we confront tragedy, it's like our lives are torn apart.**

Form a circle. Pass the tape around the circle, and have teenagers each repair the torn paper of the person on their left. As kids each repair someone's paper, have them describe one quality that person has that can help repair someone else's life. For example, kids might say, "Your patience can help when others feel angry or upset" or "Your friendliness helps people in need."

When all papers are repaired, say: **Just as we repaired each other's paper, God can repair the torn places in our lives and help us to be healers in his service.**

Have volunteers pray, asking God's help in the healing of the broken places in our lives.

CLOSING
(up to 5 minutes)

If You Still Have Time . . .

Words of Encouragement—Have kids write supportive postcards to real victims of tragedy in your church or community.

World News—Pass out recent newspapers, and ask kids to find and read about tragedies. Then form groups of no more than five. Have groups discuss how their faith can help them respond to each situation. Conclude by having groups pray for the people in the situations discussed.

BIG TROUBLE

Mayor's Report

Event:
Your city has been heavily damaged by a tornado. Many people are homeless and others are dead or injured. Power is out to a large section of town.

Reaction:
Seek a commitment of help from the mayors of cities that haven't experienced a disaster. You'll have to make your plea persuasive in order to count on their assistance. You need the help of at least two other cities.

Mayor's Report

Event:
Your city has been heavily damaged by a major earthquake. Many people are homeless, and others are dead or injured. Power is out to large sections of town, and fires are raging across the city.

Reaction:
Try to figure out why this earthquake happened and if anyone is at fault for the damage. Approach the other mayors with questions about why such things happen. Question why this had to happen to your city and not someone else's. Don't actively pursue assistance for your city, just ask a lot of "why" questions.

Mayor's Report

Event:
Your city has enjoyed a wonderful and prosperous year. For years you've worked to save city money for a new multi-purpose stadium, and now it looks like you can build it.

Reaction:
Other cities may be experiencing tragedies, but you believe it's best for them to solve their own problems. Besides, none of them wanted to help finance your new stadium! Be tough when others come to you for help.

Mayor's Report

Event:
Your city has enjoyed a wonderful and prosperous year. For years you've worked to save city money for a badly needed new freeway system. It looks like this may be the year you can build it.

Reaction:
Other cities may be experiencing tragedies, but you believe it's best for them to solve their own problems. Still, you might be convinced to help if the situation is serious. Be aware, though, that you can only help one other city if you help any at all. The other mayor must have a good case before you help with cleanup (and put off the freeway project).

WHERE'S THE GLUE?

Tragedies can happen at any moment and in any place. Sometimes they happen very close to us. But we can be a part of fixing the broken lives. In God's hands we can be a "glue" to help fix lives that are broken by tragedy. Take a few minutes to come up with healing ways to respond to these tough situations. For the first scenario, you might write how you'd spend more time with a friend or how you could help out with meals.

Write your ideas in the Healing Responses column. See how big a difference you can make!

Situation	**Healing Responses**

● A friend's mother is killed in a train accident.

● A tornado hits your neighborhood and the house next to yours is destroyed.

● A freak fire destroys your home.

● A close friend is injured in a car accident.

● A classmate's father is killed in a military action.

● Lightning strikes a friend's home, and the fire destroys everything in her room.

Table Talk

To the Parent: "Nobody knows the trouble I've seen" is a song many parents could sing. Tragedies and crises happen to most everyone, and some people get more than their "fair share."

Your teenager may be surprised to hear about the toughest times you've experienced. Tough times can put stress on faith, and teenagers can appreciate your past struggles, if told honestly. Use the following questions to help you share about tragedies and other issues that challenge your faith.

Parent

Tell about the worst natural disaster that ever happened close to you.
- What happened?
- How'd you make sense of it?
- What did you do in response to it?
- How'd it affect your faith?
- What tough time in your life placed the most stress on your faith, and how'd you work through it?

Senior higher

After hearing about disasters in your parent's life, talk about:
- the parts that surprised you most.
- the parts that changed the way you look at your parent.
- places where life seems cruel and unfair.
- things that challenge your faith most.

Parent and senior higher

Complete the following sentences:
- God's role in disasters is . . .
- When I feel depressed, my faith is . . .
- I think bad things happen to good people because . . .
- Faith can help in tough times by . . .

Together, talk about times you've been picked on or ridiculed for your faith. Then discuss the following questions:
- How do you feel when you're persecuted for your beliefs?
- How can you grow in faith when others put you down?
- What are practical ways to strengthen your faith so you can face tough times?

Read Romans 8:38-39 together. Talk about how this passage can help you feel comfort in the midst of difficult times.

WHEN OTHERS LAUGH AT YOU

Christian teenagers may not understand the idea of persecution, but they do understand what it's like to be hassled or ridiculed for their faith. They may even feel pressure to hide their faith to avoid the sneers and laughs of non-Christian friends. But kids can learn to be confident in their faith, so they don't feel ashamed when others discover they're Christians.

To help teenagers learn how to respond to people who ridicule them or hassle them because of their faith.

LESSON AIM

Students will:
- **examine times they're hassled for their faith;**
- **experience how it feels to be persecuted;**
- **discover biblical examples of responses to persecution;**
- **explore ways to cope with persecution; and**
- **pray to know how to respond to those who ridicule them.**

OBJECTIVES

Look up the following scriptures. Then read the background paragraphs to see how the passages relate to your senior highers.

In **Daniel 3:8-30**, Shadrach, Meshach and Abednego refused to worship a golden image.

Shadrach, Meshach and Abednego were in trouble with the king, who sentenced them to death in a furnace. Yet boldly they stated their strength is in God's presence with them, no matter what the circumstance.

Like the three godly men, teenagers find themselves in tough situations because of their faith. The example in this

BIBLE BASIS

DANIEL 3:8-30
ACTS 16:20-35

passage can help them find strength in knowing God is with them no matter what happens.

In **Acts 16:20-35**, Paul and Silas are thrown into prison on false charges.

Paul and Silas were imprisoned because of their faith. When an earthquake allowed them a chance to escape, they remained in jail so the guard wouldn't be killed for "allowing" them to get away. Paul and Silas' example of faith and integrity impressed the guard so much he became a Christian.

Teenagers may feel "imprisoned" by the jeers of peers. And kids may use revenge or an attitude of superiority to respond to this form of persecution. Paul and Silas show, however, that a strong faith and an attitude of love can often show non-Christians that faith in Christ isn't something to ridicule.

THIS LESSON AT A GLANCE

Section	Minutes	What Students Will Do	Supplies
Opener (Option 1)	5 to 10	**Top 10 List**—Brainstorm ways they're persecuted for their faith.	Newsprint, markers
(Option 2)		**Imagination Persecution**—Participate in a story about being hassled because of Christian faith.	
Action and Reflection	10 to 15	**Persecution Competition**—Play a game and discuss how they feel when others hassle them.	3×5 cards, pencils
Bible Application	10 to 15	**Solid Faith**—Explore scriptures about faith under persecution.	Chalkboard eraser, trash can, newsprint, light bulb, box, pencil, book, Bibles
Commitment	10 to 15	**Behind Bars**—Complete a handout, and talk about specific ways to deal with persecution.	"Behind Bars" handouts (p. 28), pencils
Closing (Option 1)	up to 5	**Support Net**—List aspects of their faith that can help them deal with ridicule.	3×5 cards, pencils, tape
(Option 2)		**Persecutor Prayer**—Pray for people who hassle them.	

The Lesson

OPENER
(5 to 10 minutes)

☐ OPTION 1: TOP 10 LIST

Form two groups.

Ask:

● **What does it mean to be persecuted?** (To be killed for

your beliefs; to be hassled for your faith.)

Give groups each a sheet of newsprint and a marker. Tell one group to brainstorm a list of the top 10 ways they're persecuted or hassled for their faith. Kids may list things such as being laughed at by other kids, or being told by teachers or other adults that Christian faith isn't logical.

Discretely tell the other group to pretend to brainstorm a similar list. But tell them to laugh at and ridicule the first group's list when it's presented to the class. Remind kids not to be crude or overly cruel in this activity. Suggest they use some of the methods on the list as part of their "attack" of the other group.

After four minutes, call time. Have kids in the first group present their list while the other group ridicules them. Then let the whole group in on your setup.

Ask the first group:

● **How'd you feel when the other group ridiculed you for your list?** (Angry; frustrated; upset.)

● **How's that like the way people feel when they're hassled for their beliefs?** (People get upset when they're ridiculed; when people are hassled for their beliefs, it's usually much more cruel.)

Have kids look at the items on the list.

Ask:

● **Have you ever been in these situations? Explain.**

● **How do you feel when others hassle you or laugh at you for being a Christian? Explain.** (Angry, because I don't think it's fair; hurt, because I think people should respect my beliefs; I don't tell my friends about my beliefs.)

Say: **When non-Christians hear about your faith, they may hassle you because they see your faith as something only weak people have or because they don't understand your faith. What can you do when you're the object of this modern-day persecution? Today we'll take a look at how you can have strong faith in the midst of ridicule.**

☐ OPTION 2: IMAGINATION PERSECUTION

Say: **I'm going to read a story about a Christian teenager named Keith. At certain points during the reading, I'll stop and ask questions about what you'd think, say or do if you were in Keith's place. As I read the story, apply the situations to your own life and think about similar experiences you've been in.**

Read "The Outcast" on page 24, pausing to ask the questions as they occur in the text. Have kids pantomime how they'd feel in the situation described. Then ask kids each to explain their pantomime.

Say: **You sometimes may feel like Keith. Our lesson today will help us learn how to respond in faith to the kinds of persecution we feel.**

The Outcast

It'd been a long day at school, and Keith was ready for the day to end. But it was only fourth period—two more boring classes to go. On his way to history, Keith bumped into Troy, the unofficial leader of the most popular clique in the senior class.

"Hey, Keith. Dave told me you might want to come to our little party Friday."

Keith tried not to show he was stunned. He'd always felt a bit like an outcast at school. He got good grades and participated in a few extra-curricular activities, but the group of kids that should've been his friends had always shunned him. This was the first sign of friendliness he'd seen from Troy or his friends.

● If you were Keith, what would you be thinking?

Keith was thrilled with the idea he might be able to associate with Troy's clique, but he didn't want to sound too eager.

"Yeah, well, Dave may be right. Tell me more."

"Well, we're going to all get high, drink lots of beer and watch porno movies. Isn't that what you Christian guys like to do on weekends?"

Troy laughed and walked over to Dave and the rest of his friends, who were laughing at Keith's blank stare.

● If you were Keith, how would you feel?

As the laughter died down, Keith wandered—late—into history class. Mrs. Shultz, the teacher, began listing on the chalkboard the names of influential historical characters: Genghis Khan; Napoleon Bonaparte; and Thomas Jefferson. It was an unusual list with one glaring omission.

"What about Jesus?"

Before the words had left his mouth, Keith wished he could've stopped them. But now it was too late. Some of the class members stifled laughs while a scattered few mumbled their words of agreement.

"Jesus was probably a real person, but much of what we know about him is myth. And in case you've forgotten, this is history class, not mythology 101."

Mrs. Shultz's response turned the stifled laughter into loud guffaws and silenced the words of agreement.

● If you were Keith, how would you feel? What would you do?

Keith shrunk down in his chair. That was the end of it—no more discussion would be heard on the subject.

The rest of the day was unbearably long. Keith began to wonder if Jesus had ever felt like this. It was undoubtedly the worst day of his young life.

Keith let out an audible sigh of relief when he finally was able to slouch down in his favorite TV chair. His mother heard his sigh from the next room.

"Bad day, huh?"

"The worst." Keith thumbed through the mail and found a letter addressed to him. It was from Julie—the girl he'd met on his workcamp trip.

"Dear Keith,

I'm glad I got to know you in Tennessee this past summer. I almost didn't go on the trip because I think those Christians in my group are so phony. You know? I mean, you don't have to be a Christian to be a good person, do you?"

Keith didn't want to read any more. He'd had enough abuse for one day.

● If you were Keith, how would you feel?

Table Talk Follow-Up

If you sent the "Table Talk" handout (p. 20) to parents last week, discuss students' reactions to the activity. Ask volunteers to share what they learned from the discussion with their parents.

PERSECUTION COMPETITION

Form two teams: Persecutors and Christians. Clear an area on the floor in the center of the room, and have teams each form one half of a large circle.

Give teams each a supply of 3×5 cards and pencils. Say: **Christians, write on each card something Christian teenagers might do as an expression or result of their faith, such as pray or go to church. Persecutors, write on each card a way to ridicule Christians or a phrase that puts down Christian faith, such as "You have to be weak to be a Christian."**

After you write on a card, read it aloud and run to the center of the circle. Place the card face up somewhere in the center of the circle. Since the object of this game is to have the most uncovered cards when I call time, you might want to cover the other team's cards with your own. You may have any number of piles of cards but only the top cards of any piles will be counted.

On "go," start the competition. After three minutes, call time. Count the uncovered cards for both teams, and declare a winner. Then sit in a circle around the cards.

Ask the Christians team:

● **How'd you feel as you tried to keep up with the Persecutors?** (It was fun; it was difficult; I didn't like it.)

● **How'd you feel when the Persecutors called out what they'd written?** (Some of the things they said made me feel bad; I was angry.)

● **How were your actions and feelings in this activity like the way Christians feel when people hassle them for their beliefs?** (Some people get angry when their faith is attacked; some people try to compete with the negative comments by responding with positive comments.)

Ask everyone:

● **Which role was easier in this activity? Explain.** (The Christians' role, they just had to come up with things that express their faith; the Persecutors' role, it's easier to put something down than to come up with something positive.)

● **What happens to your faith when people hassle or ridicule you for your beliefs?** (It gets stronger; I question it.)

Say: **The Bible contains many stories of people who've been persecuted for their faith. Let's take a look at a couple of stories and see what we can discover to apply to the situations we're in.**

ACTION AND REFLECTION
(10 to 15 minutes)

SOLID FAITH

Form groups of no more than five. Assign each group one of the following passages: Daniel 3:8-30 or Acts 16:20-35.

Give each group a different object from the following list: chalkboard eraser, trash can, sheet of newsprint, light bulb, box, pencil and book. Say: **In your group, read the passage and come up with a brief skit that shows what the passage is about. The only rule for your skits is you must use your item in some creative way. For example, if I had given you a broom, you could've used it to clean the rubble after the earthquake in the Acts story.**

Have groups each perform their skit.

Then ask:

● **How were the two passages alike?** (Both stories show people under persecution; both stories show responses to persecution.)

● **What role did faith play in each situation?** (Paul and Silas trusted God to take care of them; Shadrach, Meshach and Abednego trusted God would keep them safe.)

● **How are these stories like the kinds of persecution you face?** (We deal with people who ridicule our faith; we must trust God to help us when we're hassled.)

● **What helped the people in each story handle persecution?** (Their faith; they were with other Christians; they knew they were innocent.)

Say: **Just as you had to be creative to use the item I gave you in your skit, we sometimes have to be creative as we deal with persecution. Our next activity will help us learn ways to respond when others laugh at our faith.**

BEHIND BARS

Sometimes teenagers feel trapped by the words or actions of others. This activity will help them think of specific ways to "break down the bars" that make them feel like prisoners to persecution.

Give kids each a "Behind Bars" handout (p. 28) and a pencil. Ask kids to each complete the first part of the handout. Then have them each find the person whose birthdate is closest to theirs and form pairs. Have partners exchange handouts and complete Part Two of the handout. Then ask partners to discuss the completed handouts.

Form a circle, and have kids share some of the specific ideas they had for dealing with persecution. Then have kids each say aloud one idea they'll use when someone hassles them because of their faith.

☐ OPTION 1: SUPPORT NET

Place a bunch of 3×5 cards and pencils on the floor in the center of the circle. Say: **We all have aspects of our faith, such as patience, love for others and trust in God, that** can help us deal with ridicule. Think of the person on your left, and what his or her strengths are. Then pick up a card and a pencil, and write on the card one strength you see in the person on your left. Give that card to that person. Then write at least one more card for someone else in the circle.

When kids each have at least one card, tell them to place the cards next to each other on the floor in the center of the circle. Then have kids help you tape the cards together to form a "net." Have kids huddle together and hold the net in the center of the circle.

Say: **By supporting each other with encouragement, we form a net that can help us feel confident in our faith.**

Have volunteers close in prayer, asking God to help us use our strengths as a net to help when we face persecution and help us respond in loving ways to people who ridicule us.

☐ OPTION 2: PERSECUTOR PRAYER

Say: **Jesus told us to pray for those who despise us. And Paul and Silas showed us how enemies could be made into friends. Our closing prayer will help us think about how we can pray for people who ridicule us or challenge our faith. I'll read a prayer; when I pause, think about people you know who match the descriptions in the prayer.**

Pray: **Dear God, we pray now for those who don't understand us. (pause) We pray for those who don't know your love. (pause) We pray for those who seek to hurt us because of our love for you. (pause) We pray you'll help us respond in loving ways to those who seem against us and you. (pause). Amen.**

Have kids each go to at least three other people and tell them each one reason they'll be good at handling persecution. For example, someone might say, "Your strong faith will help you when others hassle you" or "Your patience will keep you strong in tough times."

If You Still Have Time . . .

Stephen's Shoes—Have a volunteer read aloud Acts 7:54—8:3. Have kids discuss how they'd feel if they were in Stephen's position. Discuss what's changed and what's stayed the same about how non-Christians respond to Christians. Consider giving out a "Stephen's Shoes" award to the person who has the best real-life story of putting up with modern persecution.

Stop the Skit!—Form groups of no more than five. Have groups each create a brief skit dramatizing one way Christians are persecuted for what they believe. Have groups each present their skit one at a time. During each skit, call out "Stop the skit!" at a point just before the Christians in the skit respond to the ridicule or faith-challenge. Have the actors freeze until the rest of the group can agree on a faith-building response the Christians can use. Then have them complete the skit using that idea.

BEHIND BARS

Part One:

When others ridicule our faith or challenge our beliefs, we may feel trapped by their comments. Write on the prison bars negative things people have said to you or your friends about your Christian faith. Or describe situations you've been in when people have made fun of Christianity.

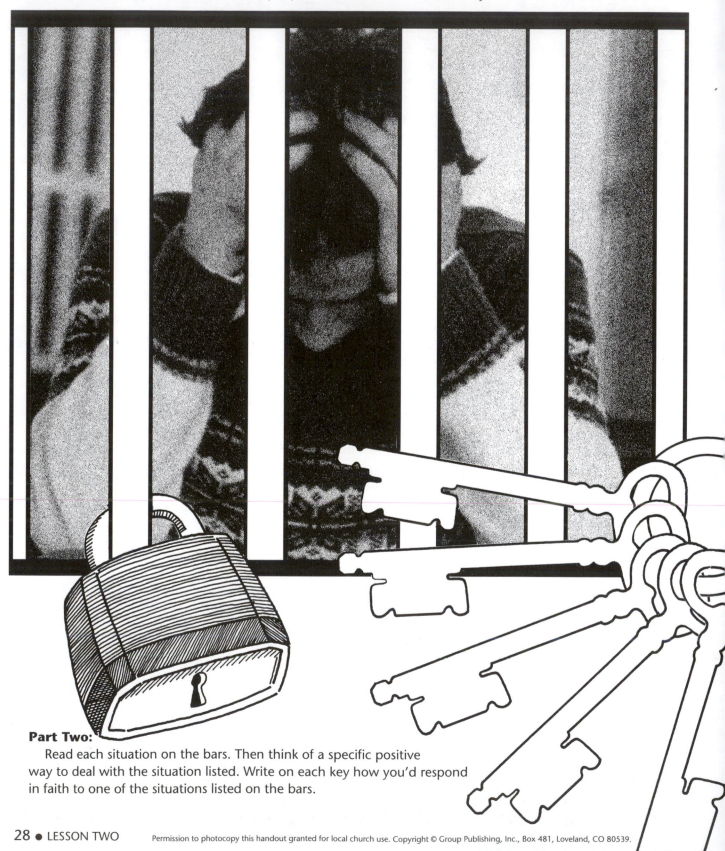

Part Two:

Read each situation on the bars. Then think of a specific positive way to deal with the situation listed. Write on each key how you'd respond in faith to one of the situations listed on the bars.

WHEN YOU FEEL DOWN

Teenagers often feel depressed. Perhaps it's because of the pressure they feel at school or the expectations they feel they have to meet. While feeling "down" isn't bad, kids can sometimes lose faith in God when they're depressed—and that's not good. Kids need to see how God can be a comfort in the down times.

To help teenagers understand how faith can help them when they feel down.

LESSON AIM

Students will:
- **explore emotions as part of faith;**
- **learn how emotions affect decision-making;**
- **identify how faith can be a strength during tough times; and**
- **experience peer support as a way of coping with down times.**

OBJECTIVES

Look up the following scriptures. Then read the background paragraphs to see how the passages relate to your senior highers.

In **Lamentations 3:19-24**, the writer recalls his pain and his hope.

This brief passage laments the pain and tragedy of the Israelites' situation. But in the end, the writer concludes that hope out of the darkness is best found by turning to God.

Many teenagers find depression an all-too-common companion. They may feel like the writer of Lamentations as they struggle to overcome their sadness. They need to know it's okay to cry out to God for help when they feel down and out—and that God will be faithful and hear their cries.

BIBLE BASIS
LAMENTATIONS 3:19-24
MATTHEW 26:36-39

In **Matthew 26:36-39**, Jesus prays at Gethsemane. Jesus expressed the sorrow of his struggle to his disciples and asked them to help by simply being there. Yet they were unable to support him in his time of need. Jesus turned to God to seek direction for his decision and asked that God's will be done. God answered Jesus' request.

When teenagers are feeling down, they, like Jesus, often turn to their friends for support. But turning to God for comfort may not be as easy or natural as turning to friends. Teenagers need to know we need God *and* friends when coping with sadness or depression.

THIS LESSON AT A GLANCE

Section	Minutes	What Students Will Do	Supplies
Opener (Option 1) (Option 2)	5 to 10	**The Blues**—Listen to a sad song, and talk about how it makes them feel. **An Emotional Mystery**—Guess feelings others portray.	Cassette, cassette player
Action and Reflection	10 to 15	**Search for Hope**—Discover how people respond to sadness and depression.	Unshelled peanuts, newspaper, small boxes, "Is It Possible?" handouts (p. 36)
Bible Application	10 to 15	**Overcoming Sadness**—Explore scripture passages to help them deal with sadness or depression.	Balloons, markers, paper, Bibles
Commitment	10 to 15	**Cloudbusters**—Brainstorm ways to beat "the blues" and grow in faith.	"Cloudbusters" handouts (p. 37), pencils, pins, balloons from Overcoming Sadness
Closing (Option 1) (Option 2)	up to 5	**A Colorful Offering**—Thank God for their feelings. **Heartstrings**—Create a symbol representing support and understanding of each other's sad times.	Construction paper Pencils, 3×5 cards, tape, yarn

The Lesson

OPENER
(5 to 10 minutes)

☐ OPTION 1: THE BLUES

You'll need a cassette of a sad song for this opener. You could use classical music, contemporary Christian music or mainstream music. Some good examples include: "Another Auld Lang Syne" by Dan Fogelberg (mainstream); "You Cause as Much Sorrow" by Sinead O'Connor (mainstream); "To Bid Farewell" by The Choir (Christian); "Hang My Head and Cry" by David Mullen (Christian); selections of classical music by Mahler, Wagner or Stravinsky.

Have kids form a circle. Dim the lights, and ask kids to concentrate on the song you're about to play. Tell them to silently think about the words (if there are any), the music and what feelings they have while listening to the song.

Play the song.

Afterward, ask:

● **How'd the song make you feel?** (Sad; angry; depressed.)

● **What about this song makes people feel sad?** (The words; the slow music; the way it's sung.)

● **Do you like feeling sad or depressed? Explain.** (No, I don't enjoy life when I'm down; it doesn't bother me much.)

● **How would you describe the feeling of sadness?** (It's like nobody cares; it's a lonely feeling; it's a scary feeling.)

Say: **Most people have times they feel down, sad or depressed. It's a natural feeling to have, especially as you grow through many changes on your way to adulthood. But how can we respond to our down times in faith? What role does our Christian faith play in dealing with depression? Today we'll try to uncover ways to respond in faith to the sadness and depression we sometimes feel.**

☐ OPTION 2: AN EMOTIONAL MYSTERY

Say: **Feelings are an important part of our lives. We get excited when our team wins a game and cry when our team loses. We get angry when someone wrongs us and depressed when we feel we don't measure up to someone's standard.**

By looking at someone, you can often tell how he or she is feeling. One at a time I'll have you come to the front of the room and express an emotion, using only your facial expression. You may not say anything or use your arms, hands or body to express this emotion. I'll tell you the emotion to express when you come to the front of the room.

Have the person whose birthday is closest to New Year's Day begin. Show that person the first emotion on the "Emotions" list in the margin. Be sure to cover up the other emotions so he or she doesn't see what's coming up. If your group is larger than 15, invite more than one person at a time to express each emotion. If your group is smaller than 15, have kids each express more than one emotion.

Have kids guess each emotion as it's portrayed. Kids who're trying to express the emotion may get frustrated. That's okay. You'll talk about their feelings after this activity.

When each emotion has been guessed, ask:

Emotions	
Fear	Happiness
Anger	Concern
Sadness	Surprise
Excitement	Frustration
Wonder	Loneliness
Depression	Embarrassment
Worry	Hate
Confusion	

● **How'd you feel as you tried to express an emotion for the group?** (Nervous; confident; silly.)

● **How's this like the way some people feel when they try to express their emotions?** (Some people have trouble expressing emotions; some people express their emotions confidently.)

● **How important are our feelings? Explain.** (Very important, our feelings tell who we are; not very important, it's what we do that's important.)

● **How do we express our feelings?** (We laugh; we cry; we throw things; we talk about them.)

● **Which feelings are the toughest to handle or express?** (Sadness; fear; nervousness; anger.)

Say: **Sometimes our emotions challenge our faith. If we're sad or depressed, we might wonder where God is during our grief. Today we'll take a look at how our faith can help us deal with some of the toughest emotions: depression and sadness.**

ACTION AND REFLECTION
(10 to 15 minutes)

SEARCH FOR HOPE

Before this activity, create a number of Hope Boxes. To create each box, wrap an unshelled peanut in newspaper, and place it in a small box.

Form groups of no more than four. Have groups each find an area of the room away from the other groups. Give groups each a Hope Box, but tell them not to pick up their box or shake it.

Say: **When we feel down or depressed we often search for hope to help us see beyond the sadness. For this activity, I want each of you to imagine a time you felt down or depressed. Take a minute to think about how you felt and why you felt that way.**

Pause for a minute while kids quietly think of their situations. Then say: **Now pretend you're still feeling down or depressed. You're searching for something to get you out of your depression. Guess what? In each of your boxes is something that can help you out of the sadness.**

Ask:

● **Do you believe me? Why or why not?** (Yes, I trust you; no, what can be in a small box that will help me feel better?)

● **What do you think is in the box?** (Money; food; nothing.)

Say: **The object has never been touched by human hands. In fact, it's never been seen by human eyes. Do you believe me now?** (Let kids respond.) **In your groups, take a couple of minutes to talk about whether it's possible for the thing I've described to exist. After two minutes, I'll ask you to vote if you believe it's possible or impossible. I'll give groups each a handout with discussion questions to help you think about this idea.**

Give some groups the top half of the "Is It Possible?" handout (p. 36). Give other groups the bottom half of the handout. Remind kids to discuss the questions with only their group.

After two or three minutes, call time and ask groups each to say whether they think the object in the box can exist or not. Once all the votes are in, ask groups if they're sure they don't want to change their votes.

Then have kids each open their box and find the peanut. Say: **Inside the shell you'll discover something that's never been touched or seen by a human, the peanut. The peanut represents the item that can help you out of your down times, faith.**

Form a circle, and ask:

● **What did you first think when I told you there was something in the box that hadn't been touched or seen by humans?** (I didn't believe you; I was curious; I was unsure.)

● **How'd the handouts I gave you help you come to a conclusion on whether you thought it was possible?** (The questions led us to believe it couldn't be possible; the questions led us to believe it might be possible.)

Say: **There were two different sets of discussion questions. One was generally positive about the possibility and the other was generally negative.**

Ask:

● **How are these different handouts like the way different people respond to your depression or down time?** (Some are hopeful; some are negative and don't help at all.)

● **How is having faith that what I said was true like having faith in God to help you through tough times?** (We have to trust that God will help us; it's tough to trust God when you can't see him; faith requires a certain amount of risk.)

Say: **Trusting God when you're down or depressed can be difficult. Just as you had to examine how you felt about what I was claiming, you have to examine how you feel about God's promise to be faithful to you. And just as the different handouts may've influenced your decisions, friends may try to influence how you respond to your sadness. Some will help you find hope; others may make you feel more depressed.**

Ultimately, you must decide for yourself what you'll believe. Yet you're not without help as you think about what you'll believe. The Bible gives good reasons for us to have faith in God during tough times.

OVERCOMING SADNESS

Form new groups of no more than four. Give kids each an uninflated balloon, a marker and a small piece of paper. Have kids each write their name on the paper and place it in their balloon. Have kids each blow up their balloon, tie it and set it aside for a moment.

Say: **In your groups, read aloud the following scripture passages: Lamentations 3:19-24 and Matthew 26:36-39. Use your markers to write on your balloons the negative feelings described by or experienced by the people in the** scripture passages. Then write on your balloon how you feel when things aren't going well or when you feel down.

Give groups five minutes to read their scripture passages and write on their balloons.

Then ask:

● **How'd the people in each passage cope with their sadness?** (The person in Lamentations trusted God to help him; Jesus asked God to help him know what to do.)

● **What do these verses say about how we can deal with our sadness or depression?** (We can trust God; we can ask God's help.)

● **The writer of Lamentations lets God know how bad he feels. Does it help us to tell God how we feel? Why or why not?** (Yes, God wants us to share what's really important to us; no, God already knows how we feel.)

Say: **Look at your balloons. When we begin to feel sad or down, we often feel like a cloud has covered us—just as your words obscure your view of your name inside the balloon. But we can learn specific ways to break out of our clouds and see hope in the middle of sadness and despair.**

Have kids put the balloons aside until they're needed during the next activity.

COMMITMENT
(10 to 15 minutes)

CLOUDBUSTERS

Give kids each a "Cloudbusters" handout (p. 37) and a pencil. Say: **We each have different ways of coping with sadness. Write on the clouds things that bring you down. Then on the sun's rays write things that can help you better handle the sad times.**

Form groups of three. Have kids share their handouts and discuss the questions at the top of the page. Then have kids each say one thing they like about the ideas each group member had. For example, kids might say, "I like your idea of reading the Bible when you feel down" or "You have great ideas on how to overcome sadness."

Form a circle, and ask:

● **What did you learn from others about how to deal with sadness or down times?** (There are lots of ways to overcome depression; we can ask God for help; we can help each other.)

Give kids each a straight pin. Have kids each hold up their balloon from Overcoming Sadness, call out one way they can overcome depression through faith, and pop their balloon.

Ask teenagers each to commit to use at least three of the ideas mentioned the next time they're feeling down or depressed. Encourage kids to look out for each other and help when things get tough.

☐ OPTION 1: A COLORFUL OFFERING

Place sheets of construction paper on a table. Have kids each select one color that best expresses their most prominent feeling during the previous week.

Form a circle. Say: **Our feelings are important to God, and God wants to be part of how we cope with our emotions. I'm going to begin a prayer, and each time I pause, thank God for the feelings you had last week and the feelings yet to come. During the pause, tear off a piece of your paper and toss it into the center of the circle.**

Begin the prayer: **Dear God, thank you for the feelings we had last week.** (pause) **Help us to see how our faith can help us when we feel down or sad.** (pause) **Give us the wisdom to seek a friend's comfort and encouragement when we feel down.** (pause) **Because we know you care about our feelings, we offer our hearts into your care and love.**

Have kids toss the rest of their papers into the circle and pray silently before you close by saying: **Amen.**

☐ OPTION 2: HEARTSTRINGS

Give teenagers each a pencil, a 3×5 card, tape and a 6-foot-long piece of yarn. Have kids each write on their 3×5 card the thing that most often makes them feel down or depressed. Then have kids each tape their card to the wall. Some kids may feel uncomfortable letting others read about what makes them depressed. Have those people tape their cards face down on the wall. Remind kids to take this activity seriously and not to laugh at what people write on their cards.

Next, ask kids each to silently take their yarn and connect it to their card. Then have them each use tape to attach their yarn to the other cards so it connects as many other cards as possible. Say: **As you connect the yarn from one card to the next, think of it as a symbol of our understanding and support for one another's sadness.**

After a few moments, call the group together. Have kids look at the web they've created with the yarn and cards. Close with prayer, thanking God for the ways we, with God's help, can help each other through sad times.

CLOSING
(up to 5 minutes)

If You Still Have Time . . .

Caring Tissues—Give kids each a few tissues and a thin-line marker. Have them each write words of encouragement on the tissues. Kids might write things such as "Hang in there" or "God is with you." Have kids give the tissues to each other as a symbol of their concern and willingness to help in times of need.

A Penny for Your Feelings—Give half your kids each a penny. Tell them they may go to any teenager who has no penny and ask, "How do you feel when . . . ?" For example, your teacher calls on you for an answer; your sister gets better grades than you; you lose a race. After kids each answer, they get the penny and ask someone else who doesn't have a penny. Tell kids to not ask embarrassing questions.

IS IT POSSIBLE?

Discussion Questions

- How could something exist that no person has ever seen or touched?
- Should you really believe your teacher is telling the truth? Why or why not?
- The teacher could be making this up just to spark discussion about trust or faith. What do you think?
- How could someone put something in a box without seeing it or touching it?

IS IT POSSIBLE?

Discussion Questions

- Surely this item could exist, couldn't it? What do you think?
- Why would your teacher go to the trouble of making these boxes if there wasn't anything special about them?
- God has created some surprising things. Could this be one of them? Explain.
- If the teacher is trying to trick you, which response do you think he or she is hoping to get? Explain.

CLOUDBUSTERS

On the clouds, write things that bring you down. Then write on the sun's rays things that can help you better handle the sad times. Remember to consider what we discovered in the scripture passages.
In your group, discuss the following questions:
- Why do some people seem down all the time?
- What can you do to help others trust God during difficult times?
- How can your faith help you in times of joy or sadness?

LESSON 4

THE SUPER FAITH WORKOUT

Christian teenagers weather tough times with varying degrees of success. Sometimes they feel their faith being tested beyond their ability to handle the situation. Other times they find great comfort and confidence in their faith. With God's help, kids can grow in faith to weather tough times with confidence and hope.

LESSON AIM

To help teenagers discover ways to strengthen their faith so they can better face tough times.

OBJECTIVES

Students will:
- evaluate various aspects of faith;
- discover how faith can be made stronger;
- develop a plan for the growth of their faith; and
- celebrate the strength and uniqueness of one another's faith.

BIBLE BASIS
PSALM 46
EPHESIANS 6:10-18

Look up the following scriptures. Then read the background paragraphs to see how the passages relate to your senior highers.

In **Psalm 46**, the author praises God's strength.

The psalmist knows strong faith means trusting God.

Teenagers sometimes feel all alone when times are tough. When kids realize God's strength is available to them, they can better work for a solution that brings peace. Instead of seeing God as the author of tragedy and violence, they'll begin to see God as the solution.

In **Ephesians 6:10-18**, Paul describes faith as a suit of armor.

This passage uses military imagery to show how we should

work to build up our defenses against things that separate us from God. The strength Paul speaks about is spiritual strength, not physical strength.

Teenagers sometimes feel defenseless when situations or people challenge their faith. They can learn from this passage how to build their "faith armor" to better face the tough times.

THIS LESSON AT A GLANCE

Section	Minutes	What Students Will Do	Supplies
Opener (Option 1)	5 to 10	**Faith Scramble**—Determine the importance of various faith-builders.	"Faith Scramble" handouts (p. 44), scissors
(Option 2)		**Faith-Steps**—Discover how much faith they have in each other during a game.	Paper, pencil
Action and Reflection	10 to 15	**Faith Workout**—Discover how physical exercise is similar to building faith.	Music (optional)
Bible Application	10 to 15	**Workout-Wear**—Read scriptures and learn how faith is like a sweatsuit.	Bibles, 3×5 cards, pencils, masking tape
Commitment	10 to 15	**Just Faith It!**—Develop a specific plan for building their faith.	"Workout Plan" handouts (p. 45), pencils
Closing (Option 1)	up to 5	**Take a Number**—Cheer for each other.	Bible, paper, marker, masking tape
(Option 2)		**Pep Talk**—Get encouragement from the teacher.	

The Lesson

☐ OPTION 1: FAITH SCRAMBLE

Copy the "Faith Scramble" handout (p.44), and cut apart the cards to make complete sets of eight cards. You'll need a set for each group of five.

Form groups of no more than five. Give groups each a set of cards from the "Faith Scramble" handout. Say: **The object of this activity is to place the cards on the floor in order of importance. Each card describes one way people can build their faith.**

Have groups each place their cards in random order on the floor. Then have kids in each group number off according to the time they got up this morning—#1 being the person who

OPENER
(5 to 10 minutes)

got up earliest. Say: **On "go," the first people in the groups may each move up to two cards in their group's cards. You'll have 10 seconds to decide and move the cards. If I call "stop" before you've moved the cards, you may not move them. Then I'll call "go" and "stop" for each person in your group until everyone's had a chance. Try to arrange the cards so they're in the order *you* want them to be by the time the last person has his or her turn. And remember, you're not to discuss the choices you make with other group members.**

After the last people have had their turns moving the cards, have groups each present their final order to the whole group.

Ask:

● **Are you pleased with the final order of your group's cards? Explain.** (Yes, we all had the same basic ideas; no, I'd have put them in a different order.)

● **How easy was it to decide which cards to move? Explain.** (Very easy, I knew which things I thought were most important; not very easy, each item was equally important.)

● **Did you agree with all the decisions other members of your group made? Why or why not?** (No, I thought other cards should've been moved; yes, the cards really could be in any order anyway.)

Say: **We build our faith in many ways including those listed on the cards. But just as this activity pointed out, we don't always know what priority to place on these ways. How can we best develop a stronger faith in God? Today we'll try to discover the answer to that question.**

☐ OPTION 2: FAITH-STEPS

Have kids each stand in a line against one wall of your meeting room. You'll need space for kids to walk forward as many as 15 steps, so you might want to do this activity outdoors or in a large room. Write #11 on a sheet of paper. Fold the paper, and don't let kids see the number written on it.

Say: **In this activity, the object is to take as many steps as possible away from the wall without going over the number I've written on the paper I have in my hand. This number is between one and 20. In order to win the game, you must end within two steps of the number without going over the number.**

Now here's the catch: You must agree as a group whether you'll take each step. You may discuss among yourselves what you think you should do and why, but you must have complete consensus before you take a step.

Ask the group:

● **Will you take step #1?**

Wait for their response, and then continue with the same format until the group decides not to take another step. Remind kids they can discuss whether they'll take another step. If the kids stop after the ninth, 10th or 11th step, congratulate them. If they take more than 11 steps, wait until they stop, and tell them what number you'd chosen.

Play the game three times, each time picking a new number and writing it on the paper.

Then ask:

● **How easy was it to decide together whether to take a step? Explain.** (Very easy, we were swayed by one person's ideas; difficult, people didn't want to risk many steps.)

● **Did you have faith in any particular person's argument? Explain.** (No, I wasn't willing to trust anyone's ideas but my own; yes, I trusted one person who had the best reasons for moving forward.)

● **How'd you feel as you thought about whether to take a step?** (Anxious; worried; confident; unsure.)

● **How is that feeling like the way some people feel when they must trust God in difficult times?** (They probably aren't sure they're doing the right thing; they sometimes rely on others to help them know what to do.)

Say: **In this activity, we experienced working together, thinking about difficult decisions and having faith in something we couldn't know for sure. Those elements are all part of our lives as we learn to have faith in God. Today we'll exercise our faith and learn to build faith in God so we don't worry so much in the difficult times.**

FAITH WORKOUT

Have kids clear an area in the center of the room. Say: **Let's take a break from the lesson. It's exercise time. We need to stretch our tired bodies and build our muscles.**

Lead kids through a variety of exercises, including toe-touches, sit-ups, neck stretches and arm twirls. Choose activities that don't make kids work too hard, since some may be in somewhat restrictive clothing. And be sensitive to kids with physical disabilities or limitations.

As kids exercise, ask the following questions:

● **Why do people exercise?** (To keep fit; to lose weight; because they like pain.)

● **What good does exercise do for our bodies?** (Builds muscle; burns fat; increases lung capacity.)

After three minutes of exercise, say: **Okay, now we're going to run a 30-mile marathon. We'll all get our running clothes and meet back here for the run. Are you up for it?**

Some kids will probably boast that they can run the 30 miles. Other kids will simply ask, "You're kidding, right?" Challenge kids to answer honestly whether they could run a 30-mile marathon after their simple exercise session.

Ask:

● **Did we work out enough to be able to run a 30-mile marathon? Explain.** (No, we need to build our endurance; yes, if you're already in shape it doesn't take much training.)

● **What would be a realistic training program for some-**

ACTION AND REFLECTION
(10 to 15 minutes)

one who wanted to run a 30-mile marathon? (Kids' answers will vary widely. Ask for specific plans including schedules for increasing running distance and exercises they'd use.)

● **How is training for a marathon like building your faith to handle the tough times?** (In both cases you need to practice; you need to build up your endurance.)

● **How can we "train" our faith for dealing with tragedies, persecution, depression and other tough times?** (Read the Bible; talk with Christian friends; pray.)

Form groups of no more than five. Assign groups each one of the following "exercises": Bible bends; joyful jumps; forgiveness flexes; love lifts; trust twists; hope-toning. Have groups each come up with an exercise motion based on their exercise title. For example, a group with "Bible bends" might practice opening and closing a Bible while doing deep knee-bends.

Have groups each present their exercise to the whole group and describe why the activity represented is important for building faith. For fun, play bouncy music while groups present their exercises.

BIBLE APPLICATION
(10 to 15 minutes)

WORKOUT-WEAR

Have someone read aloud Psalm 46. Then have kids form themselves into human sculptures representing how the passage makes them feel. For example, kids might pose as bodybuilders to show the Psalm makes them feel strong.

Say: **When tough times come, it's good to know we can turn to God for strength. In Ephesians 6:10-18, Paul describes how faith is like a suit of armor. But for our next activity, we're going to imagine faith as a sweatsuit.**

Have someone read aloud Ephesians 6:10-18. Then have a volunteer come to the front of the class. Have kids think of exercise clothing to match each of the items of armor in the Ephesians passage. For example, instead of the helmet of salvation, kids might suggest the sweatband of salvation. Encourage kids to be creative with their ideas. As kids each come up with an idea, have them write it on a 3×5 card and tape it to the volunteer in the appropriate place. Warning: If your volunteer is a girl, remind kids to be cautious about the placement of the "breastplate" substitute. Suggest they have the girl attach the breastplate item herself.

When kids have come up with ideas for all the parts (helmet, breastplate, shoes, belt, shield and sword) read aloud Hebrews 12:1. Say: **Life is like a race, and with the proper equipment and training, we can be prepared to meet the many challenges we're bound to face.**

COMMITMENT
(10 to 15 minutes)

JUST FAITH IT!

Give kids each a "Workout Plan" handout (p. 45) and a pencil. Say: **It's common for a coach to place players on an exercise schedule. We can place ourselves on a similar** schedule to help develop our faith. Complete the handout according to the instructions. Remember to be realistic and honest as you complete this handout.

Have kids work for three minutes by themselves. Then have kids each find a partner and spend another three minutes talking over their plans and refining them as necessary to make them challenging and reachable.

Ask:

● **How important is it for Christians to seek to improve themselves?** (We need to improve our faith; not very important, helping others to know God is most important.)

● **How does discipline fit into our faith?** (We need to develop good habits; faith isn't something you can plan for.)

Say: **Now that you have a plan for building your faith this next week, make a silent commitment to God to follow through on your plan.** (pause) **Consider planning a similar schedule each week as you seek to develop your relationship with God. Now let's celebrate the wonderful gift of faith God has given each one of us.**

☐ OPTION 1: TAKE A NUMBER

Read aloud Hebrews 12:1 again. Say: **If the Christian life is like a marathon—one that people around us are watching—we each need a number.**

Write large numbers on sheets of paper with a marker. Then tape a different number to each person's back.

Have kids stand in a circle. One at a time, as you call their number, have kids each stand in the center of the circle while everyone else cheers and applauds them for being a winner. For a fun variation, make up an affirming rhyme for each person's number; for example, "Let's hear it for #25, because she's always so alive" or "Let's hear it for #23, for he's so kind, don't you agree?"

Close with prayer, asking God for strength for the race of life and for faith in the tough times.

☐ OPTION 2: PEP TALK

Gather kids in a huddle, and give them a faith pep talk as if in a locker room before a big game. Use the sample below or create your own. Be sure to include a positive statement about each person in the talk. And be enthusiastic.

Say: **It's a tough world, and we're going to be thrown some hard times. Some folks will ridicule and mock us for living as Christians. Sometimes, when depression drags us down, we may feel we can't go on. We have to hang together and let God help us through. But we have the talent right here!**

Customize here to fit your group using the following example: "Ben has the strength of concern for others; Mary has the agility of being a good leader; Toni has the fortitude of a solid

---

CLOSING
(up to 5 minutes)

friend . . . " When you've said something about each person, have kids join you in yelling (in unison): **We can do it!**

Thank kids for participating in the class, and encourage them to help each other grow in faith.

If You Still Have Time . . .

Faith Team—Have kids imagine the class is a faith team. Form groups of no more than six. Have them each brainstorm an appropriate team mascot, theme song and team colors for the faith team. Have groups present their ideas, and then have kids each vote on their favorite mascot, song and colors. Ask kids to describe the significance of each team item. For fun, have someone design a T-shirt based on the winning items.

Course Reflection—Form a circle. Ask students to reflect on the past four sessions. Have them take turns completing the following sentences:

- Something I learned in this course was . . .
- If I could tell my friends about this course, I'd say . . .
- Something I'll do differently because of this course is . . .

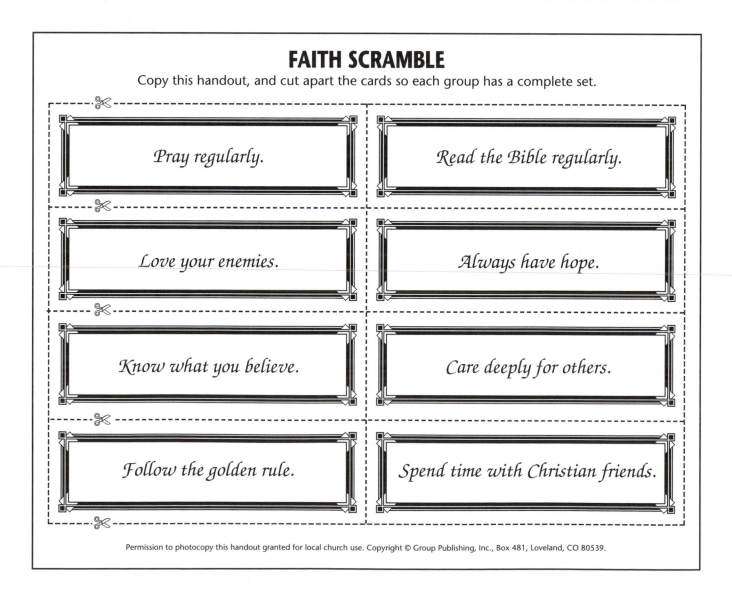

FAITH SCRAMBLE

Copy this handout, and cut apart the cards so each group has a complete set.

Pray regularly.	*Read the Bible regularly.*
Love your enemies.	*Always have hope.*
Know what you believe.	*Care deeply for others.*
Follow the golden rule.	*Spend time with Christian friends.*

WORKOUT PLAN

Choose your "exercises" from the list below. Use the space next to items to describe in detail what you'll do. Then decide which days this week you'll do them, and for how long or how many times.

Use the calendar below to help with your planning. Remember to challenge yourself in this plan. Be realistic. Don't make it too easy or impossible.

Exercises   **What I'll Do**

Read Philippians.

Read Ephesians.

Begin keeping a journal between you and God.

Write a letter to God expressing your feelings.

Write a song about God, faith or your church.

Write a poem about God or a spiritual experience.

Read a chapter from the book of Psalms.

Pray for others in your school.

Pray for people in the news.

Visit someone in a nursing home.

Draw or paint a picture expressing your faith in God.

Give something away.

Take time to care about someone new.

Spend time with your parent(s).

Do something unselfish.

Volunteer to do something good.

Find a friend and discuss your beliefs together.

Remind yourself that Jesus loves you.

Others: _____

_____

_____

Day 1:	Day 2:	Day 3:	Day 4:	Day 5:	Day 6:	Day 7:

I promise to follow this faith exercise program for the days I've listed.

Signed: _____   Witnessed by: _____

BONUS IDEAS

Tragedy Prayer Board—Provide a space on a bulletin board for newspaper stories and photographs about crises around the world. Beside each newspaper clipping, place a 3×5 card for kids to initial as a promise to pray about that situation daily.

Depression Rescue—Have the kids put together a "rescue kit" for helping people who're depressed or feeling down. Encourage kids to be creative as they create the kit. They might want to include such items as balloons, confetti, uplifting scripture verses and homemade cookies. Talk with teenagers about when the kits should be given to others.

Persecution Skits—Form groups of no more than five. Create role-plays that illustrate the kind of persecution kids most often feel. Have groups each present their role-play. Then discuss ways of coping with and responding to the situations presented.

Emotional Motions—Have teenagers develop a sign language that allows them to express feelings to one another without words. For example, happiness might be expressed as a simple wave of the hand, or sadness might be expressed as a bowed head. Then say each day of the week, and have kids express in their sign language how they felt on that day during the previous week. Encourage kids to have fun with the sign language to express feelings when they see each other.

Mo' Blues—Ask teenagers to bring tapes they like to listen to when they're feeling down. Have kids help you choose songs from each tape to play for the whole group. Then discuss the songs and how they encourage or build up people who're feeling down. Discuss how each person has different ways of overcoming sadness and depression. Encourage kids to be sure God is a part of their method for overcoming the blues.

Faith Check-Up—Have kids each complete the "Faith Checkup" handout (p. 48) and discuss it in groups of no more than five.

Table Talk—Use the "Table Talk" handout (p. 20) as the basis for a meeting with parents and teenagers. During the meeting, have parents and kids complete the handout and discuss it. Have parents and kids discuss how they feel about their faith when it's being challenged by tragedy, depression or persecution. End the meeting on a positive note, encouraging parents and kids to help boost each other's faith during tough times.

Dark/Light Party—Throw a party where the first half of the party is dark, sad and gloomy; and the second half is fun, happy and exciting. Send invitations on dark paper. Plan the event to begin after dark. Encourage kids to wear dark clothes. Set rules such as no smiling or laughing during the first part of the party.

Decorate two rooms. Make one dark and depressing. Decorate the other so it's bright and colorful. Have kids start in the dark room by participating in slow and sad activities such as sad poetry-reading, watching sad parts of movies or having a crying contest. Then have kids move into the bright room for the second half of the party to participate in fun, wild, happy crowdbreakers and games. Check out *Quick Crowdbreakers and Games for Youth Groups* or *Boredom Busters* (Group Books) for ideas. Look for activities that add laughter and help people feel good about themselves. After the party, brainstorm ways kids can turn sadness into joy.

Shelter Retreat—Plan this retreat at a location away from what's normal for your kids. If you're in a city, go to the country. If you're in the country, go to the city. For the entire retreat, have kids imagine a disaster has just occurred. Use sound-effect tapes to provide mood, and props to make the scene more realistic. Videotape fake news reports to help add to the realism!

Create role cards to give to kids during different parts of the retreat. The role cards give instructions on how each person is affected by the disaster or what role he or she will play. Roles could include a scared young married couple, a distraught businessperson or an injured doctor. Sponsors could play the roles of police, vandals and reporters. Plan specific times for kids to be in their roles and other times when they can step out of their roles for discussions.

Throw the kids some surprises, and let them make decisions about what to do. For example, at one point you might explain that the amount of air left in the building can only last a few hours. Have kids work together to come up with creative ways of dealing with the situations. Provide scripture passages for keeping hope alive in difficult times.

After the retreat, talk about what happened, how kids felt and why they acted as they did during the disaster. Ask what role their faith played.

PARTY PLEASER

RETREAT IDEA

FAITH CHECKUP

For each of the following phrases, circle the number that best expresses your response.

1—You bet!
2—Most of the time
3—Only when I feel like it
4—Not very often
5—You're kidding, right?

I turn to God for strength when things get rough at school.	1 2 3 4 5
I think about my faith when making important decisions.	1 2 3 4 5
I see God as a really close friend.	1 2 3 4 5
I'm thankful to God when good things happen.	1 2 3 4 5
I try to read scripture often.	1 2 3 4 5
I memorize verses that mean a lot to me.	1 2 3 4 5
I try to treat others as I want them to treat me.	1 2 3 4 5
I'm patient with God.	1 2 3 4 5
I try to love my enemies.	1 2 3 4 5
I pray for others.	1 2 3 4 5
I pray for myself.	1 2 3 4 5
I offer my time and effort to help out at church.	1 2 3 4 5
I let others know about my faith.	1 2 3 4 5
I have a good idea of what's right and wrong.	1 2 3 4 5
I control my actions.	1 2 3 4 5
I worship.	1 2 3 4 5
I have hope in God.	1 2 3 4 5
I can be trusted.	1 2 3 4 5
My faith is a strength to me in tough times.	1 2 3 4 5

Take a look at how you did. Did you circle mostly 4's and 5's? Talk with your teacher, youth worker or pastor to find new ways to build your faith.

Mostly 3's? Building your faith should be something you work on daily, not just when you feel like it. Read the list again and work on raising your score.

Mostly 1's and 2's? Great! Keep on growing in faith. No matter what your score, you can always grow closer to God.

Put a checkmark by the three places you feel you need the most work. Then commit to work on those areas during the coming weeks.